Dear self,

What will it take to love
you?

DEAR SELF

WHAT WILL IT TAKE TO LOVE YOU?

GABRIELLA WILLIAMS

The events described in this book are based on the experiences and recollections of the author.

To all versions of me

Thank you for your courage and willingness to go there

And for never, ever giving up.

I love you

X

Welcome

Embark on a journey of self-discovery and unapologetic self-love with Gabriella Williams' captivating book, Dear Self: What Will It Take to Love You. This compelling collection of poems and prose invites you into the world of a rebel, an indomitable spirit who dares to embrace self-love in a world that often insists she shouldn't.

With her eloquent and touching words, she crafts a narrative that's as much about self-acceptance as it is about defiance. Each piece in this collection is a mosaic, beautifully piecing together the complex and often challenging journey of loving oneself amidst external disapproval and internal doubts.

Dear Self doesn't just tell a story; it's an experience. It's about finding beauty in one's imperfections, strength in vulnerability, and courage in being true to oneself. Gabriella's verses are a soothing balm and a fierce battle cry all at once, echoing the sentiments of anyone who has ever felt at odds with themselves or the world. This book is more than just a collection of words; it's a companion for those nights of soul-searching, a guide through the winding paths of self-realization, and a celebration of the resilience of the human spirit. It's for anyone who's ever questioned their worth, fought their demons, and is in pursuit of a love that begins from within. Join Gabriella Williams in this intimate, transformative exploration.

Dear Self: What Will It Take to Love You is not just a book; it's a journey towards embracing the true essence of self-love and the power it holds to change our lives.

Intro – Self what?

I had no idea what it meant to love myself. Like so many of us, I was brought up to believe that it wasn't something people do. That indulging in self-care and things that made me feel good or happy, was disapproved of and seen as selfish or wrong. I was taught that it was important for us to put others' needs before our own in order to be accepted as a caring and kind human being; that playing by the rules made you a good and well-mannered member of society (WTF?!). The only thing that created was a lifetime spent feeling used, abused, worthless and never good enough!

This wasn't something ever demanded of me, nor pushed on me by my parents growing up. They were loving and generous and provided all they could and more for me and my sister (and still do). But they were also trapped in these very same patterns of behaviour, believing what society tells us what we should do and who we should be. I always knew I was loved and that was never in question. I was also raised to care deeply for my family and those around me, but I never witnessed in any shape or form what it meant to give that love to ourselves. Most of my understanding of the wrongness of this came predominantly from the outer world. From school and media, other family members, friends, rules, demands and expectations, and such a limited and un-encouraged space to ask questions. To be able to challenge the things that didn't feel right or true, or to be allowed to think for myself.

I'm now thirty-four as this book is coming together to be shared with the world, and I can honestly say, despite many years of self-reflection and inner work, it has only really been in the last few years that I have begun to truly form an understanding of what it actually means to love, honour, appreciate and gift to myself. And, more importantly, to do so without judgement. However, as I reflect back on the willingness and awareness I've had, to want to change things in my life since I was in my early twenties, I realise I have always in some shape or form been trying to get to this space. Whether I fully knew it or not.

I've never bought into the illusion that there are quick fixes to all of life's challenges. Or that you learn a lesson once and that's all it takes for the rest of your life to be utterly amazing. But neither have I bought the illusion that nothing can ever change and life is just the way it is. That we are stuck with the cards we've been dealt. From a very young age this has always sat heavy with me, despite never being able to do much about it until a lot later on. Nor understand the true power we hold to actually make these changes. Instead, I see life as a continual work in progress, and each new space rewards us with something different, such as an awareness or level of joy or gratitude we didn't have before. Given the lifetimes of conditioning, as well as time we've spent learning the very opposite of what is acceptable for us to have, do and be, it can often take a lifetime of undoing and unlearning in order to return to a sense of peace, clarity and oneness within ourselves, and with the world around us. I don't believe life is about reaching a destination, but instead being present to all the gifts available to each of us in every moment. And the possibilities and experiences that present themselves when we are willing to be more of who we truly are.

Each time I find myself reaching a new space of awareness, one that gives me more clarity or a deeper connection to who I am, I am blown away all over again by the amount of lightness and space it creates in my world. And the miracles that often occur as a result. I eventually realised that we can go to all the therapy and spiritual sessions or classes we want. We can ground ourselves, meditate, listen to music that has empowering lyrics or read various books that tell us what it means to love who we are (at least from each individual's point of view), but what it really comes down to is choice. It's something we have to be willing to choose for ourselves every single day, regardless of what the outer world decides is right or wrong. It is something we have to consciously and continuously put the effort into practising, creating and being, in order to actualise it. And it starts by communicating with our beautiful bodies and listening to its needs. Being in constant question and recognising what truly feels good for you as an individual and then asking yourself, "Okay, what would it take to have more of this?"

Loving yourself in a world that tries to convince you it's wrong is most definitely a rebellious act. And I don't know about you, but I found that I kind of like being a rebel and creating a sense of mischief and chaos! As well as the idea that I can play a part in unleashing a level of love and potency that is so powerful, it might actually just change the world one day!

This new awareness around choice has excited me more than anything else I have discovered over the past few years. Mostly, because it changes things almost instantaneously by putting the power back in our own hands. Yet the simplicity of it is often overshadowed by the belief that choice is not something we are allowed to have, and the fear that that creates by going against what we have been told is acceptable. So, by choosing differently and in daring to change these beliefs, it prompts a new way of being that allows us to break free from the cages we have been placed in, the limitations we have chosen to stay safe within, and the rules we have always assumed we had to follow. It unlocks a level of power that has the capacity to make some significant changes in the world, if enough people were willing and brave enough to choose it.

So, are you willing to acknowledge the unlimited potential you have within you to rediscover and re-awaken your magic and all that you are?

Are you willing to be a rebel and make a choice to love yourself exactly as you are? And from there explore what else is possible?

If so, then please keep reading. It is my hope that this book may contribute in some way to help expand your awareness. Inspire, encourage, activate and perhaps open a doorway to you truly being and loving you.

Part 1

A willingness to heal

I embarked on a more conscious healing journey back in early 2019, during what I would describe as the most painful, messy and worst time of my life! Yet it was also the most powerful and transformational. I use the word conscious because I believe in many ways I'd been unconsciously building up to this significant breakthrough, or greater awareness, for several years prior to this - mostly by making a number of different choices that went against the advice and guidance of those around me.

One of those choices was to seek a more holistic-based approach to address the painful, physical and emotional conditions/issues that had robbed me of the majority of my late teens and twenties. A determination to 'find another way' became the driving force that led me to explore the real reason behind the symptoms that had been controlling my life since I was a teen, and to find a way to heal them.

I'm not a huge fan of the word 'spiritual awakening', but for want of a better phrase this is exactly what I believed happened. I eventually reached a higher, or perhaps just different, state of awareness of life and self, that was triggered by the harsh and blunt force of hitting rock bottom. Where it felt like the very foundation beneath me had completely disintegrated and I finally surrendered to the knowing that things needed to change.

Little was I aware at the time that my willingness to heal and to change the projections and limitations that had been placed on me by others, would lead me on a path that would challenge everything I thought I knew; would strip away even more of the life I had always known, and push me to face things that were so painful I realised I didn't really know what broken was until I experienced the real trauma of acknowledging unhealed wounds that were buried under years' worth of Band-Aids. This also gave me an awareness of the harm this was causing my body and how it was actually more painful pushing these things away and resisting them, than it was in finally allowing it all

2

move through me. And it was essentially this which had contributed to my body getting sick. Through this process of surrender I was gifted with yet another significant awareness; that I wasn't in fact breaking down as I had thought I was, I was breaking open. And I was finally allowing all that makes us human to be seen, heard, felt and even loved.

What happened after this changed everything. Because I was now aware of the control we give to the ego mind, society, and those we give our power too, and the veils had been lifted. Instead, a space opened up for me to explore a whole new way of being and seeing the world, and the role I was to play in it. Rather than feeling alone and isolated, and trying (unsuccessfully) to be the hero in my own story and that of others, I knew there was something more. A team. A universe of unlimited possibilities that was ready and waiting patiently to co-create with me. And my life was only just getting started!

Despite the disruption this created in my world, which can be common when things are no longer congruent and in alignment with who we are and where we're headed, I now knew I didn't have to face it alone. And the more I surrendered and let things happen, the more space opened up for new possibilities to emerge. With each step taken and the choices made so far, I have learnt, or more so, *remembered*, something about myself that I hadn't given space to before. I have found a courage to explore, a confidence to embrace and a vulnerability that allows me to delve deep into the places and areas of my life I never once would have dared venture.

It's taken a lot of work (and still does) to step out of my comfort zone, to listen to and honour my own truths, stay neutral to the opinions and judgements of others and just show up as myself; especially when that side of me had been shut down for so long. But the bravest part in all of this has been to face up to the fears I'd bought of rejection, separation and judgement. To look into the mirror at the woman now staring back at me, who for years I had avoided and believed to be unworthy, and to finally ask what it would take to love her.

All of her.
All versions.
All layers.
All levels.
Her too much-ness, her weirdness and everything I once thought was wrong.
And then to open my heart to her and truly listen.

Letting go of control

I've been sat on this book, or the idea of it at least, for several years now. It started as one thing and changed many times as I slowly and patiently accumulated the pieces of something I felt was meant to be shared with the world one day, but with no idea when. I have lost count of the times I've had to surrender all expectations of what I thought it would be and look like, and instead allow it to surprise me and have the space to form in its own time. There have been many moments of frustration when I've found myself wanting to be in control and to get it finished, and yet there has also been a beautiful lesson involved in actually letting go, and allowing something to organically come together as it's meant too. It has felt like a long and slow process, but a necessary one, as I too have had to honour all I have experienced that has enabled me to put these words to paper – as well as recognise that the world may not have been ready to receive it until now. It's humbling to think that as this reaches the hands of those of you who are called to pick it up, or even those it's been gifted to, that the words on these pages may contribute in some way to weaving the magic of all that we are out into the world – through connection, recognition, vulnerability and love, and the power that each of our stories has when we witness and share them. Not from a place of definition or attachment, but awareness, potency and empowerment.

When I find myself in a space of healing or growth and I want to express or put words to what's going on in my world, and share what I'm feeling, I find most of what comes through does so in the way of poetry. Much of what I have written over the years hasn't been seen by anyone until now. I had no idea they would one day become part of a collection of musings that I would share within a book. This is an example of just one of the expectations for how the book would be, that I found myself having to surrender. None of the other ways I'd attempted to write out what I thought wanted to come through seemed to work. Nor did I wish to simply fill a book with all the tools that have helped me over the years. Especially when they have come from so many different sources and many beautiful people who have already spent time and energy sharing them.

The pieces I have shared or that have been written and gifted to others have been received with such love and kindness. They have allowed me to witness the power that words can truly have, and this is mostly what prompted me to approach the idea of this book in a different way. One amazing friend who showed up at exactly the right moment to help with this, gifted me the awareness one day that all the poetry that follows is the book I'd been attempting to write all this time. Over a period of around five years the book had already in fact been written, I just hadn't realised it until then. These pieces are my story and my journey of healing. Each express a deep vulnerability, rawness and drive to move through some of the most challenging experiences of my life, which I hope have the capacity to also inspire others. And gift a sense of comfort and courage to those who can relate to them.

The magic of being weird

Part of learning to love myself has also meant allowing myself to be seen, and stepping out of the shadows that I have spent the majority of my life hiding in as a result of feeling too much and shut down from such a young age. I became very good at shapeshifting into who everyone required me to be, and to blend in within a space that never actually allowed anyone to really know me at all.

Yes. I was a chronic people pleaser! But hey, I've learnt to love her too.

From a young child, I danced continuously between being too much or not good enough, as I tirelessly tried to figure out how to fit in and know the 'right' way to be. I had a wildly curious mind and a vast imagination that was never nurtured when I stepped out into the world and started school. I spent several years fighting for this part of me to be acknowledged, (which was often mistaken as me 'acting up or misbehaving'), because I wanted to believe there was space for magic and possibilities, and children like me who I soon realised saw the world so differently. But each attempt was rejected or ridiculed until I was beaten down so much that I finally surrendered into the role of the obedient (yet quietly frustrated) little girl, who was expected to conform and play by the rules. Feeling like I had no other choice at that age, that's who I became. I had no interest in core subjects that didn't excite or inspire me, nor allow me to learn in a more creative way. But I struggled through it all just to get the grades and passes I needed to finally free myself from the education system. My love of creating was the one main thing that kept me going, and was a way in which I was able to express the part of me that longed for freedom.

I spent the entirety of my school years tormented by endless bullying. Despite my attempts to try to blend in, I always seemed to find myself a target. The very fact that I tried so hard to be accepted, was what only made me stand out even more. I was uninterested in fashion or make-up, partying or the latest trends. I loved making things, spending

7

time outdoors, being around animals, my grandparents and usually always had my head in a book. (It was my way of escaping, and being and experiencing what I thought I couldn't be in the world. In a way it also nurtured my imagination so that I never truly had to shut it down). I was definitely a weird kid, but I so wish I could have told her what I know now and that her weirdness was in fact her magic. Though I like to think that maybe a part of her knew, and that's why, despite all she went though, she gathered up and saved what she could of it, knowing that one day in the future the time would finally come for us to unleash it. And that maybe the world would be ready to receive it by then, too.

Who am I?

When you spend so much of your life adjusting who you are to suit others and blend in with the world around you, there eventually comes a time when you realise you don't actually know who you really are. Where you get so used to the roles you've become accustomed to playing, that you lose yourself completely. And everyone else's beliefs of you feel so real that even you begin to believe them too. In nearly every relationship or friendship I've experienced, I found myself giving up so much of me, that by the time I finally reached breaking point, I had no idea what was true for me anymore - what I liked or what actually made me happy. At one point I even had the belief that I didn't know I was allowed to be.

Part of a promise and commitment I made to learn to love and give back to myself has involved a huge amount of exploration and self-discovery, in order to begin to call all parts of me that were once lost or rejected back home again. And it's been during this time where I've learnt to develop the most beautiful connection and communication with my body; a relationship that has taken a great deal of patience, tears and time to build trust with again after resenting and rejecting it for so long. I held so much blame for all the pain and problems I believed it had created in my life growing up, when in actual fact my body had only been trying to look after me and protect me from all the shit I had taken on.

In my early twenties after being diagnosed with both endometriosis and fibromyalgia, I reached a peak of pain that no longer allowed me to function day to day. My body at this point was literally screaming at me to take notice and it was no longer something I could ignore. I am so grateful in a strange way to the doctors and medical professionals I saw during this time, who were so uninterested in helping me to get well again, that it pushed me to take matters into my own hands and seek alternative ways that I could heal my body. Some part of me knew it was possible and I genuinely love the inner warrior in me at that time who was stubborn enough to fight for something different.

Rather than give up and succumb to simply existing and spending the rest of my life in and out of surgery, and taking high doses of medications and pain relief, I was determined to find another path that not only allowed me to heal and reclaim my health, but also understand why all these problems had arisen in the first place.

I spent the entirety of my twenties seeking a variety of natural therapies such as acupuncture, hypnotherapy and kinesiology, all of which contributed to me being able to begin to shift some of the trauma held in my body. Rather than save for my future or spend money on holidays and nice things, I worked as much as my body would allow me to, to earn what I could to pay for the treatments and care my body required instead. It was a level of self-care I had no actual awareness of at the time, but that I thought I was just choosing because I wanted things to change. I took notice of my diet and the foods I was consuming. I made changes to my job and work situation so that I could carry on doing something I loved, rather than having to give it up entirely as I was told I would have to do. I began to adjust my entire life in order to listen to my body and its needs and willingness to heal if I was ready and prepared to do whatever it took to work with it.

I still had to endure several operations over that time and many setbacks, but as my body was getting stronger, each recovery got shorter and easier until I no longer required that kind of intervention. By the time I reached my thirtieth birthday, I had not only reversed the fibromyalgia diagnosis completely, but had significantly reduced the symptoms I had been getting from the endometriosis, and I was able to finally start enjoying life again. For the first time in a long while, I felt like I *had* a life and so much of that came from being willing to go beyond the symptoms I was experiencing, and explore energetically what was being created in my body.

The physical side to healing was just one part, the other was a deep dive into the world of self-reflection, emotional trauma and generational wounding, which is definitely not for the faint-hearted!

This exploration pushed me to see all the places I was not only creating this in my body and my life, but also choosing it, and so I had to confront a lot of demons and uncomfortable truths during this time, as well as clear the imprints of literal demons and ancestral baggage that I had picked up along the way or brought with me to address in this lifetime. It has definitely been brutal at times, but the awareness and freedom it has enabled me to create in my body and my life has been worth it. And it's given me a whole new perspective on what it is to love and appreciate the body and space we occupy during our lifetime spent on earth. Not only that, my world has opened up to so many more modalities, miracles and possibilities which are available to all of us to work with, and that we can use in partnership with our bodies. I know in time I will be able to achieve the level of health and healing I know is possible, as well as play a part in sharing it with the world.

I wouldn't be where I am today without the incredible people that have shown up in my life over the years. Some as if by magic when I needed it most, and others that I believe were placed on my path at just the right moment. Those who have worked with me, walked with me, shared with me, supported me, inspired me and helped me to get to the space where I am now. Each have contributed nuggets and gifts of wisdom, healing and nurturing spaces for me to feel safe to explore and make the shifts and breakthroughs I've been able to make. I am truly grateful for each and every one of them and the parts they have played in my life, and friendships and connections created as a result.

It's okay not to be okay

Often when we embark on a more spiritual journey, or open up to more awareness even, people assume that means you have to be full of love and light all the time, and in a constant state of peace and harmony. I've had some very interesting points of view cast my way around this over the years, and as much as it would be lovely to be in such a high-vibe state at all times, it unfortunately isn't how it works, at least from my experience! Yes, you still have good and bad days. Yes, you still get your ass kicked, and yes you can most definitely still hit rock bottom. Many, many times! In fact, this seems to happen even more regularly when you show up and take responsibility for your own life and healing, and as you continue to go through multiple phases of shedding and releasing all that no longer serves you; as well as building and re-building your foundation over and over again until it is in full alignment with who you truly are – which can be pretty disheartening, especially if you didn't see the cracks until it was too late!

The most challenging part I've found with this is when it follows those moments where you feel as though you're really making headway. When you're more connected, alive and finally life is just getting good again. Then suddenly, the next level of healing comes in and gatecrashes the party, wiping you clean off your feet. I will admit, I have often wondered during these moments why we bother showing up to do the work at all, and put ourselves though this time and time again! But it eventually passes, along with my frustration at its rude and ill-mannered timing when I then see the gift it actually was. More often than not it's saved me from something that wasn't actually working out in my highest interest (even if I didn't want to believe it at the time!).

As well as the experiences that knock us down, there are also the times where we can find ourselves stumbling into what feels like a dead end. Where we forget our 'why' for a moment and seem to have wandered off the path we thought we were on, only to find ourselves some place that we weren't expecting. These moments I find particularly disorienting and challenging, and they usually arise for me following a time of feeling good and being in flow which then suddenly seems to fizzle out. Yet I have often found these experiences to be really important as they have either happened to remind me to take a break, to rest, recharge or go have some fun for a while if I've got a little caught up in healing something particularly deep. Or, it's because there is something I need to know that's usually preventing me from moving forwards. I love the saying that goes 'sometimes we fall down because there is something down there we are meant to find'. This can often be a really significant insight or gift of awareness that creates a huge breakthrough if we are willing to ask the right questions, and be in the discomfort of stagnation for a while.

At the end of the summer of 2022, I experienced my third miscarriage within a period of nine months. The year had been filled with a mix of hope and heartbreak, but a determination that this was my year to have a baby - especially after having spent so long working on my health and preparing my body to carry a child. All the signs were there and the timing of it all had just felt right. Having gone through several years of fertility issues and unsuccessful IVF rounds with my ex-partner, I decided the year following my divorce I was going to try for a baby as a single woman. It was a huge decision, but one that came with an incredible amount of support from my family and friends. I felt empowered to be choosing this path on my own, knowing that I wasn't ready for another relationship any time soon, but having children was something that had been a dream of mine for as long as I can remember. With the support around me, I was reassured I wouldn't be raising a baby alone and I knew that so many people would be a gift in contributing to his or her life. My longing to be a mum had been at the forefront of the healing journey I had embarked on in recent years, and so, after a lot of research and decision making, I found a donor and started fertility treatment.

Every time the pregnancy failed to hold, and despite being crippled in pain from each excruciating bleed that then followed, I continued to wipe my tears, pick myself up and keep going. After three attempts, none of them resulting in a pregnancy that was able to stay more than a few days, I finally reached a point where I had to stop. Financially, as well as emotionally, I had reached a limit, and yet I desperately wanted to keep going. This time, however, I listened to my body as I'd been learning to do and chose to honour myself by taking a break to heal. Up until this point everything had felt so positive. I felt like I was in a great space physically and emotionally and that I was ready for this new adventure, so I couldn't understand what was going on. All I knew, given my previous history, was that this had now broken me on a whole other level and was about to kickstart an even deeper level to my healing. I wasn't expecting it to also birth something a little different than planned into the world, one of which you are holding in your hands.

Upon surrendering all plans to fall pregnant in 2022, I just allowed things to be as they were for a while, and I focused on taking care of my body and staying open to whatever came next. In doing so, I ended up signing up to a kinesiology training course after a prompt from another therapist. I knew this was a sign from the universe and so I took notice of where I was being guided to go and started something new. For a long while I was becoming restless and bored in a career I'd been in since I left school, so although this new path had come a little out of the blue, I was also excited by it and eager for a change. Weirdly, I also felt like this was linked to the healing I had asked for in order for me to be able to try again for a baby in the future, and a way of me deepening my connection to my body and my fascination around this particular healing modality. Yet, despite the feelings of excitement by this new venture and where it might lead, I also found myself struggling to fully embrace it because it now felt like I was having to make a choice. Training in this field can take several years and be costly, so I had to come to terms with the idea that either an opportunity would present itself for the two dreams to somehow work together at some point, or I would have to wait until I qualified and get settled in a new career before I re-visited my options. Letting go of a dream this huge has been incredibly tough. The not knowing when and if still feels unbearable at times, but it's also taught me a lot, especially around surrendering and trusting where I am.

As with most of these kinds of courses, a big part of the training is based around self-healing. I knew it was going to be good for me, but I had no idea of the depths it was going to take me to. No amount of kinesiology sessions in the past had prepared me to go to the level I found myself going to, and it was here that I knew the real healing had begun.

Sat among strangers who would soon become friends, I slowly began to open up, something that has always been a bit challenging for me. But the safe space we all created for one another, held by the most amazing tutor and mentor, allowed me to reach a level of vulnerability I had never gone to before. As we set our intentions for the course and first weekend, and were asked to share what we wanted to work on personally, I found myself sat with one of the most uncomfortable, unexpected and possibly most difficult realisations I'd experienced so far. When my turn came around to share the affirmation that I intended to work with over the course of those few days, I found myself admitting (for possibly the first time in my life) with tears rolling down my face as I looked up at the group and said,

"It's okay for me not to be okay."

The true power of what I had just admitted hit me as a wave of emotions that I had been burying the past ten months (and from years' worth of unacknowledged trauma) rose to the surface. I hadn't realised just how much I had been convincing myself I was okay and how brave and strong I was to keep getting up and carrying on despite the losses and struggles I had gone through. It was how I had learnt to be over the years and define myself in order to survive. Yet in that moment, I finally understood the real bravery had come in admitting that actually I wasn't okay – I was angry, heartbroken, lost, confused and it hurt like fucking hell.

Stepping out

Years' worth of trauma from childhood bullying to the loss of my grandparents, the breakdown of my marriage, health issues and fertility heartbreak led to me being unable to feel safe in my own body. Despite wishing I had more of an awareness of this earlier on, (I have also been reminded time and time again that all things happen when we are ready for the next level of our growth), I didn't fully understand until many years later that a huge part of my own healing would require me to relearn how to be present. 'Stepping out' was my trauma response and I'd got so good at it that I was barely living from a space of true presence anymore.

Prior to my 'spiritual awakening', this hadn't been much of an issue. In fact, for the majority of my life it had mostly served to keep me safe. But when being spiritually aware and awake means becoming fully present to everything, this was where I began to notice certain things were more challenging. When a lot of teachings guide or encourage us to sense our own energy, become mindful and aware or to tune into all that's around us, the beauty, colours, sounds, etc., and to really ground our roots into the earth and feel centred, I realised no matter how much I seemed to try or however good an intention I set to anchor in, I just never got that sense of peace and calm that comes when you surrender into a state of pure alignment and being.

For me, I felt like I was here but not here. Aware but not fully engaged or present. Never completely in each moment and living a lot of my life on auto-pilot. Sometimes it literally felt like I was standing just to the side of my physical body, wanting yet unable to step completely back in. The more I began to notice what was happening, the worse it seemed to get because even with an awareness and a willingness to change this, no amount of meditation practices, energy exercises or grounding techniques seemed to help. What I hadn't realised at the time was that I *was* in fact slowly healing this, and being shown the steps I needed to take to address it, they just hadn't been what I was expecting; and that it was going to take time to retrain my body and nervous system to feel safe to experience the things I wanted to experience without going into fight or flight or freaking out. The biggest awareness I was gifted from this was the realisation that if I didn't feel safe to be in my body, then how was a baby going to feel safe to be in it either.

This is where I've come to truly love this work, (despite its often interesting and frustrating challenges) and where I still believe it's totally worth it, even during the toughest times. Because I'm always being reminded and surprised by just how supported and held I am, and that everything, even the things we find difficult or the days we think we've ventured off path, we are always heading in the right direction. There is always some bit of magic to be discovered that will get us back on track and encourage us to take the next step. There are always more possibilities if we are willing to ask for something different to show up.

Feeling everything

At the beginning of 2023, I was really feeling the collective heaviness of the energy that was slowly starting to shift from the past few years. January for me has never been a time of empowerment or filled with excitement or enthusiasm to set goals and begin new projects. It's usually cold and wet and a time where I have to really take care of my own energy to ensure I don't get lured into the heaviness that seems to linger at the start of each year. I see January as a time where we are still meant to be cocooned in the latter phase of winter, slowly beginning to stir but not yet ready to emerge. That time for me comes in spring, when the first signs of daffodils begin to gift us with their welcomed burst of colour and the lighter evenings allow for more time for inspiration and exploration. The spring of 2023 definitely felt like it was going to be powerful too, full of big shifts and energetic changes. But, when the beginning of March came and the sunshine started to warm up the surroundings, as did the daffodils, I still found myself unable to emerge from hibernation. It didn't feel like the big shift I had been preparing for. In fact, I wasn't sure I wanted to come out of hibernation at all. Everything around me at that time had started to become louder. My senses felt overly heightened and everything seemed to overwhelm me. Despite doing continuous grounding and cleansing practices, I seemed to feel and hear everything on a whole other level. My body felt like it was in a state of constant fight or flight and all I craved was complete silence and isolation.

I have always been a fairly sensitive person, particularly when it comes to sounds. As a child, I would wake at the slightest noise and I'm often able to hear things that most people wouldn't even notice or pay attention too. These types of sounds are usually categorised by the brain as just background noise, and although they were things I was often more aware off, they were suddenly really loud and triggering a huge amount of anxiety. I began noticing that things like having the television on with the tumble dryer going in the kitchen, whilst someone was also having a conversation on the phone, and all of this taking place in different rooms throughout the house with the doors shut would still somehow send me into a rage of irritation and overwhelm. So much so that I was ready to scream. I was beginning to feel like I'd taken a huge step backwards considering I'd been working on so much of my own healing at this point. I couldn't bear being in public spaces, I struggled to be around more than one family member at a time or meet up with larger groups of friends. It felt isolating and uncomfortable and what was worse was even the sounds of things I usually loved, like the birds outside my window or the sound of my cat purring next to me was too much. I have never craved utter silence like that before and all I wanted was to mute the world for a while so I could calm my frazzled nervous system.

More than ever, I was noticing this resistance to being present and in my body. The slightest sound was making me 'jump out', and so I eventually began to get curious with it. I knew this was happening for a reason and my body was trying to make me aware of something. I just needed to create space to listen (which was a little easier said than done given the noise sensitivity!). Each time I found myself in this space of overwhelm, I started to pay closer attention to what noises I could hear that seemed to have triggered me and also the emotion coming up. From the way in which I was reacting each time this happened, I was becoming aware that it was creating a much deeper emotional response, rather than the sound simply being irritating. One of the most significant reactions it was prompting was anger. Deep raging, wanting to scream at everyone and everything, kind of anger. And within it I felt extremely unsafe and fearful. Just the thought of being with it felt too out of control.

Anger was one of the emotions I had yet to explore during my healing sessions – and perhaps one I had admittedly been avoiding. It seemed like it was now coming to the surface and letting me know it was ready to be witnessed and the time was right to address it. But, as much as this felt like a relief in the sense of being ready to confront and heal what was going on, I was also aware this emotion ran deep and had a lot of ties to some pretty painful experiences in my past. So, I'm not going to lie, the thought of coming face to face with this stuff frightened the shit out of me.

Anger was also something I had always been scolded for expressing and had never been given the space to let out when needed. There are many moments where I remember being shut down by others, unable to voice my own thoughts or feelings and being left with this simmering rage at being misunderstood or invalidated and, at worst, being told to calm down and shut up!

One of the links I made with all this arising was the sound of one of our dogs barking. Surprisingly, considering I have grown up with and have a love of dogs, this seemed to be my biggest trigger. His low tone, loud and continuous bark when he was outside in the garden prompted the most overwhelming rage that made me feel like I was on the verge of a panic attack. I felt like I couldn't escape it and I was scared to be with it or release it. What was more interesting was that this feeling felt very familiar, yet I couldn't understand why it was being triggered by our dog.

I took this to one of my healing sessions with a fellow kinesiologist, at this point desperate for some help before I completely lost my mind and turned into a female version of the hulk! It was within this space that I was able to begin to further explore this feeling of anger and start to make sense of the links. The familiar feeling was from a time in my marriage where things had become very toxic and unhealthy. The arguments we were having were full of rage and mixed with our own unhealed baggage that meant we were unable to find any way past the blame and hurt that we were holding onto and projecting. Again, a pattern for me was played out by having my feelings invalidated and, despite asking for time out for us to process what was going on and calm down, I was never given the space to breathe, reflect and be alone for a while so that I could regain a state of clarity or sense of self. This led to feeling unable to escape situations which often triggered a panic attack and a complete lack of safety or respect for my own needs. All the while this was going on, the neighbour's dog was often outside in the garden barking. It appeared my brain had linked these events and sounds together and this was what was being triggered by my own dog barking a few years later, creating the same familiar feelings and emotions that had yet to be dealt with. This is one of the reasons why I find all this so fascinating as our bodies truly are always communicating with us, if we will only listen!

During my personal kinesiology sessions, I finally allowed myself to sit with this emotion. Having someone hold space for me to do this was a big deal for me, but it was incredibly helpful given that it was such a big one to process. Letting myself feel this emotion out in relation to where it had come from was uncomfortable to say the least, yet the more I sat with it, the more it seemed to soften somehow. I began allowing it to flow, as opposed to holding onto it so tight and burying it down, and gifted myself permission to be with it. This exploration allowed for some really interesting insights to come forth that began to completely change the way I looked at anger. It was always something I never felt like I could express without judgement or being told it was wrong, yet I came to realise that my anger had also played a role in keeping me safe and had been supporting me many times throughout my life. It had been the driving force behind the courage I finally found one day to walk away from my marriage. To have the guts to tell all the things that weren't supporting, kind, loving or positive in my life to fuck off. Without that burning rage to keep reminding me I deserved better and that I was in fact worthy and deserving of love and happiness, then I probably would have stayed where it felt familiar and safe on a materialistic level because I didn't know I could make another choice.

I'm incredibly grateful to the badass, don't-fuck-with-me feminine warrior who emerged in burning flames of anger and rage during that time, and I genuinely owe her a lot. In truth, I'd go as far as to say she actually saved my life.

And that's how I came to understand anger, to stop being afraid of her or to push her away. Anger became a friend, an ally, someone I knew I could rely on in a more positive way, and trust to keep me safe. I finally respected the role she had played in my life and learnt to love her. But what was even more beautiful was that I discovered later on, this hadn't in fact been anger at all. It was potency.

What was really interesting by relating this back to the noise sensitivity, was that so much of the noise I was experiencing was actually coming from others. When I listened to the opinions of others the noise grew louder; I felt more overwhelmed and sensitive and the further away from self I got. When I learnt to let go of this and to listen to my own thoughts and feelings, and validate them for myself, I found the silence I craved. I got more clarity about who I was, found the peace I needed to be still and the more I learnt what it was to be present. I could then sit with what I felt and actually feel it out or ask it a question. Presence came from recognising that the external noise was simply a distraction, and often from those around me who were projecting and weren't yet willing to look at what was going on in their own world. I was finally able to be present when I listened to myself and asked what I needed in that moment, then took action to positively and healthily release my emotions.

This heightened sensitivity to sound it turned out was in fact not a burden, but a gift. When I feel things in my world beginning to get louder and I'm suddenly emotionally triggered in some way, I know it's an indication that either something within me is coming up to be processed and released or there is something my body requires. That's my cue to find some space in my day to go and sit with the emotion arising or to drop my barriers down and allow it to move through me; to check in and see if it's even mine, ask it a question or use a tool to shift it out of my energy field. It's also a sign that there's a lot of external noise that's influencing my thoughts and actions, and I need to retreat for a while to find my truth and centre again.

When we really do take time to listen and be in question, our bodies can truly gift us the most magical awareness for creating change.

Empowered

So, this is where I hand over to the next part of this book. A space filled with words and poetry, thoughts, reflections, awareness and magic. This first part has hopefully created a bit of context for where these words that follow have come from. For they reflect the spaces where I found vulnerability, where I could process big emotions such as grief, and how I learnt to open up and to let go. Where I found courage and bravery to be more of myself and discovered so much about who I am beneath all the layers and years of conditioning.

Loving me is gifting me the ability to show up more in the world and to keep breaking free from all limitations and beliefs of lack. The last thing I was told when I walked away from my marriage was that no one was going to 'put up' with me and all of my issues. But he couldn't have been more wrong. Because I decided in that moment that that role belonged to no-one else but me. It was my responsibility not to 'put up with' as it was projected, but to actually be the love and compassion for myself that I had never truly known. And it was the greatest gift of acceptance, love and freedom I have ever gifted to myself. This was triggered by reaching a point one day where rather than accepting the conclusion that this is what my life had to be, I instead decided to ask what it would take to change it and love myself instead. It opened up doors of possibilities I had never known were there or available to me before. And that is where the magic lies; in our willingness to choose, to change and to ask a question – to always be in the question, because there is always more available. It's about being willing to know what you think you don't know. To bravely be what you think or have been told you can't be, and to let the miraculous universe show up in ways beyond what our humanness can comprehend.

I truly hope this contributes in some way to igniting the rebel that lies within us all, and the magic, potency and light we hold which is meant to be shared not buried, hidden or tamed.

Because loving you is the greatest gift you can be for you and also for the world, and it is needed now more than ever before.

xxx

Part two

- Always
- Done
- Letting go
- Grief
- Who am I
- Growth
- Surrender
- Pace
- Wings
- Unknown
- Shattered
- Pause
- Beginnings
- Witnessed
- Whole
- Acceptance
- Legacy
- Plot twist
- Planted
- Power
- World
- Reminder
- Journey
- Rise
- Courage
- Fire

- Light
- Silence
- Everything
- Loved
- Universe
- Magic
- Potency
- You
- Soul sister
- Back to being
- Walking home
- For you

Always

You knew,
And that's all that mattered in the end.
When I couldn't find the words.
When I could no longer fight the tears.
When I felt my heart breaking as I tried to imagine what life was going to be like without you.
But you just took my hand one last time and you squeezed it tight, like you always used to do when I was little.
And in that moment no words were necessary.
Because I felt it.
Because the love that we shared said everything that we wanted to say.
You looked up at me and smiled
And in the silence of our goodbye
Both our hearts whispered
Always

Done

Enough
She was done
A line crossed
An end met
A full stop in this story
She collected up what was left of her bruised and battered heart
The battle scars she hid and the pain that had finally brought her to her knees
The unknown of what came next terrified her
Along with the uncertainty as she walked out of a life she had become so accustomed too
Knowing there was so much she was going to have to let go and surrender
So much to say goodbye to that would further break her heart
But the life she had built had been slowly crumbling for some time now
And she could no longer ignore the destruction happening around her
Staying in a space that was destroying her soul was now too much to bear
Though she knew it was going to cost her dearly
That it would take losing everything that was left in order to find even a breadcrumb of hope that would guide her back to herself again
She owed herself that
So she followed the tiny spark of worth that had shown up at the end of the road
It promised of more yet gave little away of what awaited
But it whispered of a new beginning and a fresh start
So she gathered up her courage and took a step
And stumbled out of the life she had been barely existing in
She let the walls cave in and the windows shatter
She allowed the foundation to crumble and disintegrate beneath her feet
There was no going back now
Not now that she saw the truth
Not now that the illusions and lies had been exposed
Not now that she had made a promise to herself to seek something better
That she deserved the happiness and love she craved
For lifetimes she had chosen others and always put them first
She had bowed to their needs
Conformed to their demands
Silenced her voice and her dreams for too long

And given away too much of her love in exchange for acceptance and a false sense of belonging
But this time, right in the middle of life as she knew it
Before she lost herself entirely
She made a different choice
And she chose herself instead
Even if it meant losing everything to find her again.

Letting go

What does letting go mean to you?

How does it feel?

What does it look like?

Do you feel an empowering sense of release as you shed a layer of your being? Like a heavy winter coat you no longer need as the seasons transition into spring.

Do you envision bagging up all your old and unwanted belongings and feel the satisfaction of giving them away to be renewed and recycled.

Perhaps letting go is more subtle, just a brush of a though like a ghost that passes through you with a shiver, and then vanishes as though it was never there at all.

Are you someone who feels every emotion as if you're saying goodbye to a lifelong companion? Taking time to ride the waves and navigate the stormy seas of change.

Does it feel like the welcome release of a burden that you've finally set down as you take off the heavy rucksack from your shoulders?

Or maybe you envision a part of you breaking free, soaring into the skies until it becomes invincible to the naked eye.

Letting go can be a process that occurs when we choose too or feel we are ready, and sometimes it can happen when we least expect it. When we need a little nudge and the universe steps in to offer its help.

It can slip out in the middle of the night without so much as a goodbye, leaving only the whisper of a memory, yet you can no longer remember the face. A photo album that's now filled with only black spaces, ready for a brand-new adventure.

Letting go can happen at any place, any time, any moment. In the middle of a sentence, a release of a breath, a jump into the ocean, a walk in the woods, a trip in your car or in your deepest moments of solitude and reflection.

We can encourage it like a child ready to fly the nest. And yet sometimes we still find ourselves holding on. Sensing a flicker of resistance and nervous uncertainty that creeps in to test your courage.

We can embrace letting go when we feel a calling for something new. In those moments where the journey ahead feels exciting but there isn't enough room in the suitcase to take all that you own.

We can sometimes fear it, when it has such a hold around our heart that it leaves us wondering if the void it creates will ever be filled again.

It can drive us on when doubt creeps in and for a split second you hesitate before a quiet voice whispers, go on, do it anyway.

Letting go can be beautiful and exhilarating, and it can be messy and painful. Sometimes it can be all of them at once. Like some kind of abstract masterpiece of emotions if they were ever to be painted on canvas.

But in letting go there is always a promise of growth and opportunity. Of a new beginning.

There is treasure to be discovered when space is created to allow one to receive its magic.

Letting go is a silent inner victory, an unbinding of chains and contracts, a triumph for the brave, a light in the dark and a blanket of encouragement for the walk into the unknown.

Whatever it is for you, let it go.

Grief

What is grief but a heavy heart that just wishes to be held.
A bag of rejected emotions, desperate to be felt.

What is grief but an empty space, once filled with a beating heart.
A room that's lost its warmth, and comfort in the dark.

What is grief but a journey through shadows, where we forget to turn on the light.
A day that feels like it's been stolen, by a cold and endless night.

What is grief but a thought left unspoken, a message never returned.
A promise made and broken, or a difficult lesson learned.

What is grief but a memory we cherish, now both bitter and sweet.
That we add to our collection of treasures, and the sentiments that we keep.

What is grief but a photograph on a shelf, that time isn't able to touch.
So that we never forget the details, of someone we loved so much.

What is grief but the surrender of a vision, a self we abandon on the road.
A way to unburden our troubles, an attempt to lighten our load.

What is grief but a body that ages, no longer in its prime.
The changes we struggle to embrace, a new self we try to find.

What is grief but a heavy silence, a ghost we all claim to have seen.
Yet we often reject its presence, in the hope it will eventually leave.

What is grief but something we fear, and will often try not to show,
But what if grief was actually just love
That simply had nowhere to go.

Who am I?

Can any of us really answer that question?

Is there even a proper answer?

Am I what happened to me and the things I've experienced?

Am I how I have been raised and brought up?

Am I a daughter, a sister, a partner, a friend?

To be these things would have to mean I am something or someone because of someone else. And therefore suggests I cannot be without these things defining me in some shape of form to make me who I am. Does that not make me a label? Or that my identity does not solely belong to me but to something external. Yet were any of these things to be removed or to change, I would still exist, so who would I be then?

So perhaps who am I is not the question we should be asking ourselves, but rather who do I want to be?

The power of the self lies in having choice and the freedom to choose what we desire in any given moment. As well as the freedom for it to continually change.

If this is the case then our identity is not in fact a thing or a label but a constant shift of evolving choices that we make, that one way or another encourages us to become the best version of ourselves we can be. And so maybe the real question lies in not limiting ourselves to being just one thing, but embracing all the different possibilities we can be.

The true value in that means we get to wake up every morning of our lives and ask;

'Who do I want to be today? And what else is possible?'

There is such an immense sense of empowerment in such a choice. And perhaps bravery in choosing it. But also knowing that even if you mess up, there is always the opportunity to choose again.

Every day is therefore not so much a second chance but a whole new day of endless possibilities which enable us to grow and expand our awareness.

Asking 'who do I want to be' gifts you the power to be the creator of your own life and essentially gain an understanding of all the ways in which you can be you.

Being open to the idea that who you are can always change and that you are never one thing or one way or limited by only the family you grew up in or the experiences you have had.

How amazing is it that we get to be that flexible. And how exciting to know that the possibilities of who you are, are actually infinite and endless.

You get to decide when you wake up in the morning to be happy,
Kind, compassionate, creative, expansive, loving, courageous, worthy,
successful, joyful, playful, and everything else in between.
The more consistent you are with choosing for yourself and getting a sense of
what lights you up and feels good to be, the more you are able to let go of a
need to be defined and to know exactly who you are, and instead can just be
who you are free of any kind of judgement.
It comes down to what you as a being are willing to choose, and who you are
willing to be in order to have the life you want to create.
A life that brings ease and joy and allows you to confidently step up and say
to the world...
Right now this is me.
Tomorrow it may change,
But today, in this moment, this is who I am. This is who I am choosing to be.

Growth

Growth occurs as a result of everything we experience.

In every moment when we choose how to respond and who we are as a result of all that's going on in our external world.

Events you never predicted can surprise you, shatter you and break you open. Things can change in the blink of an eye.

Magic can occur when you least expect it and abundance can flow in right when you are about to give up.

The key to understanding growth is to be present to all of these things.

To grow through all that challenges you the most.

Because growth is a beautifully messy process of shedding and unravelling all the layers of who you have been, in order to come home to who you truly are.

And then getting to decide who that is in every moment that follows.

It's a space of self-acceptance, forgiveness and remembering.

Because real growth actually requires you to be nothing other than yourself.

Surrender

Sometimes the real miracle is not always in receiving what we had planned or hoped for, but in the gifts we are given amidst what we often consider to be our most painful moments. Those which actually shatter and break us open to greater truths and awareness. Eventually it exposes everything so that we are left bare and naked, with nothing but light pouring in through the cracks. A full and sometimes messy surrender of self, when once our resistance subsides, returns us to a state of oneness and pure being. Only from this space of openness can we truly know what it means to belong. To know our truth and power and trust unwaveringly in the path before us and all the possibilities that await. Until then we follow the breadcrumbs and try to make sense of the signs and guidance seeking our attention. And we piece them together to gain some kind of clarity and direction. We delve headfirst into the experiences gifted to us along the way and piece by piece we fall apart. Only in the end to find ourselves whole.

Pace

Your growth is your growth, just as your journey is your journey. Our end goal may be collective, but the path we take to get there differs and that's why it's so important to remember we all walk various roads that lead to different experiences. We all choose to bring something to the table that contributes to something far greater in the end, even when it feels small or insignificant.

Therefore do not measure your rate of success or growth with that of another. When you do so it diminishes the light you came here to shine and the gifts only you can bring. Your own healing and individual lessons enable you to strive towards being the best version of yourself you can be. To be true and authentic and accepting of who you are so that others can do the same. To remember who you are and who you've always been beneath the layers of conditioning.

Rather than worry you aren't achieving, progressing or healing fast enough, instead acknowledge the wisdom that you hold. The compassion that you've created for yourself, the courage you mustered during the storms that taught you how to navigate raging seas. Refrain from judging yourself and others for where you each may be. Recognise the importance of what there is to learn and the choices we each make to stay or to change.

Be compassionate and forgiving of the actions and decisions everyone makes knowing there is freedom in recognising there is no right or wrong way to be. That in any moment others can only meet us where they are.

Hold your own lane, dance down it, run on it, crawl if you want to or pause to acknowledge where you are and actually just how far you have come.

No matter where you find yourself, we are all exactly where we are meant to be.

Shining, inspiring, growing, learning, guiding, illuminating and walking each other home.

Wings

We have such a fear of the unknown. Especially when the future has no guarantee.

And yet it is the not knowing that in a way creates our future.

It's jumping in regardless of the fear and opening up to the possibilities that present themselves when we let go of our limited points of view and allow ourselves to be surprised by the possibilities that present themselves in our moments of action and willingness to change.

That means fear isn't in fact a block after all, but a stepping stone in order for us to take a leap of faith.

The bigger the dream the greater the fear may be, but so is the magic that awaits.

It's trusting in the knowing that even if you fall, you'll learn something significant on the way down. During the decent is often where we face our fears head on, learning the most valuable of lessons.

And it's usually in the midst of it all, mere moments before we think we are going to hit the ground, that we suddenly discover our wings.

Unknown

Step gently dear one, into the unknown.
It's not something to fear, nor must you walk it alone.
You are loved and surrounded, held tight and so dear,
You have nothing to hide and no one to fear.

Have courage dear one, raise your head high.
Release and surrender, the how and the why.
Like a lioness spirit, dare to be brave,
When you don't know the road, we will show you the way.

Forgive dear one, yourself most of all,
Shed layers of your being, like the trees in the fall.
For the old slowly dies, to welcome the new,
Come home to yourself and remember your truth.

Shine bright dear one, allow yourself to be seen.
Step out of the shadows, of who you have been.
You need not be fearful, be bold and be bright
For there is room for all stars to sparkle each night.

Step gently dear one, into the unknown,
Trust the path that you walk, will eventually lead home.
Enjoy every moment, dance wild and be free
Reawaken your magic and all you can be.

Shattered

Don't be afraid of the shadows
Of falling
Failing
Reaching the end of a cycle
The walls cracking or crumbling down.
Surrender to it all brave soul.
Let the light seep in through the cracks
Watch the flowers begin to grow through the openings and all the spaces in between.
Embrace the rebirth of all that you are
See the beauty in everything you have been
And all you are yet to become.

Pause

Sometimes when a moment feels heavy and just showing up is taking all you've got. Know there is great bravery in recognising the opportunity that's being offered to you.
To pause
To notice the imperfections
To sit and find stillness in the storm
To acknowledge your feelings
To ask a question
To take a breath
Or to allow yourself to simply be where you are.

Beginnings

A year of many endings,
The wrapping up and closure of chapters.
Saying goodbye to loved ones. Letting go of people, places and parts of myself and my past that have no place in the next one I am about to write. This year has taught me a great deal about who I am and filled me with an enormous sense of gratitude for the lessons and experiences I have come through.
In the surrendering of it all it has enabled some truly beautiful things to emerge.
New friendships. Better relationships. Deep healing. A sense of empowerment, inner peace and a worthiness I have never known or allowed myself to claim before.
There is a certain magic that comes from wading through all the chaos and emotions of challenging times, and acknowledging the rawness and truths that trigger with painful endings.
For they are often disguised as new beginnings. The illusion falling away when we are brave enough to truly look at the value of these moments with dried eyes and a heart that has been bravely allowed to stay open.
There is great strength and resilience to be found when you call upon the gift of courage and get back up to write the next part of your story.
The one you realise you were always meant to write.

Witnessed

I sat with fear today
And gave her space to breathe
I listened to her worries
And all she's scared to be
I opened up a space for her
No judgement on my part
So I could truly witness her
With a loving open heart

Then I sat with sadness
And held her as she cried
I watched her as she fell apart
And gently dried her eyes
As she softened into my arms
She released a heavy sigh
Letting go of so much pain
That allowed her to say goodbye

I made some room for anger
To shout and rant and scream
And safely let out all her rage
While finally being seen
In this space I listened
And allowed her to have her moment
Which gifted me the awareness
She was actually being potent

Shame and guilt turned up next
So I gave them both some time
What surprised me when they shared their thoughts
Was that they were not even mine
The burdens they had taken on
To ensure a sense of wrongness
Was in fact a lie to keep me small
And unaware of my strong-ness

Joy was waiting to the side
Patiently awaiting her turn
It had been a while since she'd been seen
Or her voice had actually been heard
Now the others had made some room
She had space to come and play
To share the magic she could be
And the miracles of each day

Happiness emerged from the shadows
And she danced and sang in delight
Brightening up the world with colour
Her light now shining bright
She twirled and moved so free at last
To be everything she is
In a space that actually welcomed her
And allowed her to exist

When we make room for all we are
And allow nothing to be rejected
No thought or emotion can be too much
When none are left neglected
All we are is so much more
Than we allow ourselves to be
And when I gave each one some time
I knew then what was truly me

Whole

Under the full eclipse moon my soul light emerged before me, along with my shadow. All of us meeting before one another for what felt like the first time. I watched as my soul gently lifted the chin of my inner darkness, seeing and witnessing her for her bravery and strength. And as my shadow reached out her hand in return, to touch the light she had always feared, the two of them suddenly surrendered into a deep and longing embrace. Light began to pour in through tiny holes in my shadow, like a million stars in a night sky, and a swirl of darkness grew inside my soul as she made room in her heart with unconditional love and compassion. In that moment they merged as one. Together, seen and acknowledged and held.

And I have never felt so whole.

Acceptance

We spend so much time searching outwards, trying to find ourselves, who we are, where we fit in and belong. Craving acceptance for our own uniqueness and individuality, and more often than not we cut away and re-shape this in order to fit in with those around us. All the while becoming even further from the self we truly are. We believe our journey through life is to experience as much as we can, see as much of the world as possible, make something of ourselves, learn from our mistakes, find love and fulfilment, and yes these things expand our ideas of who we are and gift us experiences that can bring us joy and pleasure along the way. But are we truly present to them? It isn't until we are brave enough to venture off the path we've always travelled on, question the things we've always known, and begin to let ourselves become the way we've always wanted to be before the world told us who we had to be. When we let the true essence of our being emerge without judgement or fear of acceptance, we recognise this was the point all along. The growth was actually about growing back all the parts of ourselves we cut away, discarded and rejected. The healing was about nurturing all of you back to life. The expansion was about stepping into all that you are and the gift this can be in the world. All along its been about growing, being, loving, and not needing to be anything more than your unique, individual, imperfectly-perfect, amazing and beautiful self. And that the only person that ever actually had to accept her was you.

Legacy

Owning your story without letting it limit or define you. Stepping into all that you can be despite judgements or disapproval. Loving all parts and versions of you, even those that feel broken battered and out of place, and being able to let go of what has been in order to open up to what can be, are among some of the bravest things you'll ever do.

Healing begins the moment you step out of your comfort zone and recognise the choices available to you. The possibilities you didn't see were there, the doors that are open to adventures beyond what you once thought possible. What you were once made to believe were only dreams or fantasy.

Be your own example, shine your own light, be the kindness you wish to see in the world and bring back the magic by embracing all of your weirdness and potency. Recognise there are no limitations and boundaries to being the infinite being that you are.

Only from here can you move out of survival mode and begin to live rather than simply exist. Where you not just own your story but direct it and choose what's written on the pages.

Be the hero, the heroine, the goddess, the badass, the wild child, the magician and even the unicorn!

Be the inspiration in your own story and make that your legacy.

Plot twist

She was exhausted of being the characters in everyone else's stories.
Having to play roles chosen for her with little room for change, growth or creativity.
In some she was made the villain, and in others a saviour that was always unfulfilled and which was frustrating as hell when it turned out they didn't actually want to be saved.
She was tired of waiting for the happy endings that always seemed to be out of reach or thwarted by the love of drama and unending doom and gloom.
Fed up of being handed the script and told the lines she was meant to say and the way she was expected to behave.
How things should be rather than all that they could be.
She longed to tear down the walls of the theatre and expose the illusions and false lighting that blinded people to the truth.
To let the daylight seep in and reveal the shadows that kept everyone stuck in a space of such fear, yet were merely a silhouette which everyone once handed their power over too.
She wanted to show people there was so much more. So much more space and room for imagination and possibilities beyond the scripts written for them and the lines of conformity and limitations.
And that there was an expansiveness that could hold everyone's magic a million times over.
So in a moment of rebellious bravery, which was perhaps also encouraged by a little mischief and sheer impatience courtesy of her grandmother. She decided to yell PLOT TWIST! Right in the middle of the current scene.
She quit the roles expected of her and instead committed to saving her own damn self.
She climbed on her unicorn, with ruffled hair and little belongings other than a battered open heart and a pocket full of courage and strength. She gripped onto what little magic she had left, which she'd been saving for this very moment.
And right then in the middle of the story, no longer caring who stayed and who joined her, or the judgements she knew would follow,
She took off into the unknown and rode straight off the fucking page.

Planted

They told her to hush and whisper
Her voice was far too loud
So she let herself be silenced
And lost amongst the crowd

They told her to stop caring so much
People don't want friends like that
It makes them feel inadequate
So she held her loving back

They said she mustn't dance around
For others will mock and frown
So she sat and watched in silence
And let her enthusiasm drown

They said her imagination was too intense
And her dreams weren't valid or right
So she shoved them away inside a box
And obediently dimmed her light

They told her she had to slow things down
Her mind was chaotic and busy
That all the ideas she wanted to create
Were impossible, useless or silly

They said her energy was stifling
That she was just too much to bear
So she crammed herself into a cage
And no one seemed to care

They told her she wasn't smart enough
And probably wouldn't go far
Her best didn't really count for much
So she lowered down the bar

All the while she re-shaped herself
To what the world required

Playing obediently by the rules
Yet slowly growing tired

For when you bury down these things
That make you who you are
One day there will come a point
It won't all fit inside the jar

Cos magic cannot be contained
Least not for very long
And all who have this special light
Weren't made to actually belong

A time will come eventually
To take life back by the reins
And unleash a power deep within
So the entire game can change

For they thought that they had buried her
Her obedience taken for granted
But what they failed to realise
Was instead she had been planted.

Power

There is such a profound moment of understanding that comes when you realise that everything in life is a choice. Every decision you make, every thought you think and every action you take.

When this fully resonates and sinks in, that in itself can be one of your biggest awakenings, because you suddenly get a sense of your own power. And you see just how much you have given it away.

We can spend so much of our lives searching outwards for validation and fulfilment. Passing blame, getting stuck in victim mentalities and feeling defined by everything and everyone around us. And in every moment where we take on the beliefs of others or get stuck playing a role in someone else's story. When in fact if we are willing to be present to the truth, however uncomfortable and confronting it may seem, it all comes down to what we choose.

No one can make you feel something unless you allow it,

No one can judge you unless you receive it,

No one can make you do something unless you agree to it.

And no one can control you unless you choose to hand over your power.

You didn't come here to live a life like that.

You came here to be you.

And that power has always been yours.

World

In a world that keeps telling you who you should be and what you should do.
Seek your own truth and choose to be courageously you.

In a world where others judge, reject and try to make you feel like you're
doing something wrong or are unworthy.
Accept yourself and all that you are.
Be for yourself what you need in each moment.

In a world where there is so much divide and chaos,
Be brave enough to forge your own path and walk it, even if it means going it
alone for a while.

In a world that sometimes feels hopeless and heavy,
Find something to be grateful for, starting with yourself and just how far
you've come.

In a world that makes you feel stuck and restricted.
Ask what else is possible and discover what new doors can be opened.

In a world where things don't feel right or aren't what they seem.
Don't be afraid to ask questions, seek your own answers and find your own
truth

In a world where it's easy to get lost and caught up in the chaos.
Pause where you are and ask what this moment is trying to show you

In a world that feels dark and scary,
Lean into your shadow. Go bravely into the places within that scare you the
most, and find your light by healing and loving those wounded parts of you
that have gifted you the courage you have today.

In a world full of confusion and uncertainty.
Be the leader and an example of the love and hope that is possible by
embracing all that you are so unapologetically, that it gives permission to
others to do the same.

In a world full of people who are walking many different paths, experiencing different things and finding their own way through, have compassion and know that everyone is exactly where they need to be.

In a world where you can be anything. Where the only control you have is over your own choices and actions, choose to lean into love. To be kind, compassionate and forgiving, even through the toughest and most challenging moments knowing those around you can only meet you where they are.

In a world full of souls, remember where you all came from. That you are here to simply experience the vastness of who you can be, and remember the wholeness of all that you truly are.

Reminder

Dear self

I know all that you've been and I love you anyway.

I'm here right where you are and you are more than enough.

I have seen who you become and let me tell you a secret, it's beyond what you could ever imagine.

So believe in yourself and keep going,
Because I see you,
I've got you
I love you
And in case you need a reminder today...
You're doing great,

xox

Journey

Through your own journey and exploration,
May you find the courage to embrace who you truly are.
To go within and find that power and potency that resides deep within your soul and wake it up.
May it open your eyes to show you all you can be and shine like a beacon that guides you to reach your fullest potential.
May you choose not to fear the unknown but instead welcome it in as though it were a friend, calling you on an adventure and walking beside you on your journey of discovery. Allowing it to bring magic into each and every moment, and encouraging you to surrender and trust the path you are on.
May you find wisdom and inspiration along the way, which ignites that fire burning within you that longs to create and expand.
And surprise yourself with just how much you know and are capable of achieving.
May these ideas open up doors of opportunities beyond your wildest imagination, and stir a desire for more.
And may you find your worth in all that you are and all that you bring to the world, so that you truly believe you are worthy of joy and happiness.
May you find a reason to smile in every waking moment, and light up your life and that of others with the sound of laughter and celebration.
So that even on the days where you may stumble, that glowing light will shine bright enough to guide you back home.
May you make a silent promise to yourself that from this moment on, you will choose not to exist but to live? And to do so with enthusiasm, passion and excitement.
May you live out every single second as your authentic and beautiful self
Unapologetically
Unconditionally
And in unwavering wholeness.
And may you find gratitude for all that you are, exactly as you are and in all the blessings that surround you.
May you find peace and serenity simply by surrendering all that no longer lights you up.
And know the true meaning of belonging when you choose to love yourself instead.

Rise

I call forth the element of fire
Invoking the spirit of flames
Igniting the sparks of my soul
A fire that can no longer be tamed

Inviting strength as I let go of burdens
The courage to cut cording's and ties
Dissolving the veils of illusions
That separate the truth from the lies

I let go of negative attachments
Forgiving a past I once knew
For when I surrender all limits and patterns
It allows me to birth something new

I lay down my fears as an offering
My doubts and all limiting beliefs
Setting them free to dance in the flames
Taking with them my pain and my grief

I surrender myself to the fire
Letting it roar and swallow me whole
Cleansing, clearing and purifying
My mind, body and soul

As the fire burns down to embers
I emerge and unfold my wings
Feeling free as I take to the skies
And let myself soar on the wind

I glance back at the world below me
And smile as I ascend up high
The world once witnessed me fall
But now's my time to rise

Courage

Sometimes what feels like the right path, isn't always the easiest one. In fact it's usually the hardest because it requires a certain amount of courage that calls on you to venture into places that are unknown and uncomfortable. It pushes you to step out of your comfort zone in order to reach greater heights and overcome challenging terrains. To veer off on a path less travelled, heeding the call of a new adventure, despite not always knowing where it may lead or it tainted by the lack of understanding and judgements from others.

During those moments when there's no one else around, and you find yourself stumbling and questioning the decisions you've made. You begin to understand the importance of looking inwards. Of trusting, nurturing and holding yourself up until you find your feet again. Because walking your own path means doing so with sole responsibility, unapologetically and compassionately.

You know there will be those that show up and walk beside you, those that will cheer from the side-lines or watch from a distance, and those that may take a different direction at certain crossroads or even move off your path entirely.

You will meet new souls along the way, and lose some that no longer contribute to your journey, nor you theirs. And when this happens you learn to flow, to allow, to let go and to find peace and gratitude for the time that was once shared. You continue on, committed to your path no matter how painful it may feel.

That deep rooted trust you begin to find in yourself and where you're going, unearths new strengths and blesses you with inspiring new views and surroundings. It makes you feel brave and humble, especially during the times you spend in quiet solitude and deep surrender. When you have nothing but blind faith and trust in the journey.

I believe those are the moments that make you, and that eventually lead you back home.

Even if they break you first.

Fire

There was a spark that ignited in her.

And it began to dance and flicker, from a soft penetrating glow to a roaring burst of flames.

But like the seasons it went through times of fullness and moments where it was nothing but glowing embers as the dust and ashes were swept away in the wind.

In its state of retreat she learnt to stoke it softly, becoming aware of what the stillness and solitude had to share with her.

These moments tested her patience and the silence at times felt unbearable and lonely as the light dimmed and cast nothing but shadows. But a spark would every so often ignite just to let her know it was still there. When it did, she hoped it would dance again and that it would stay a little longer than before. That the inspiration it gifted her would be more beautiful and exciting as the last. For each time it would teach her something new.

But it would return to a state of calm once again, and as it did, she patiently returned to tending to the flames. Breathing into the space and learning to admire its beauty, even when it seemed as though it was nothing but glowing coal.

She talked to it as she would a friend, with gentle encouragement and compassion for the way it held on. Never once wondering if it would eventually burn out.

That faith was unshakable, and a part of her she had yet to fully realise how incredible it made her.

For even during the times when the tears fell and threatened to dampen the fire, all she had done to keep it going shone through, revealing its trust in her. This allowed for great growth to occur so that when the fire finally took hold once more and a spark caught and began to expand into the full force of its creative beauty, its energy roaring and ready, she knew the time had finally come.

It was a union based on trust and faith. A bond forged over time that had become unbreakable. For she had proved her loyalty and finally understood what it meant to soften, to surrender and to be.

Now it was ready to dance and to move. She felt its vibration as it began to ebb and flow. It was time to share its fullness with the world once again, only this time was different.

It was filled with a determination so passionate that the fire reached up to the skies, its warmth rippled across the planet, its light touched those she never even expected it to reach.

On and on it went, infinite and abundant. And during this time, something even more incredible happened. Other fires began to respond and ever so slowly the world began to light up. Embers were igniting and joining in the colourful dance. Feeling inspired and empowered by it all and the gifts and the story that was being shared.

A story of great bravery, wisdom and courage. One that revealed such strength when she walked into the darkness with nothing but an ember of light remaining. But trusting and releasing all fears, knowing somehow she would be okay. Then emerging the other side, engulfed in the fire that she was. Taming it, becoming it. And finally appreciating the gift that had been given to her when she followed the path into the unknown.

Her admirable endurance that never allowed her to give up and which led to the greatest gift of all.

Coming home to who she was.

Light

I woke inside the darkness
Called to by a flickering flame
Delicate and determined
Yet dimmed by guilt and shame

I followed as it danced around
Mesmerised by its glow
A gentle touch of warmth
Like a beacon guiding home

Up out of the darkness I slowly rose
And shed a heavy skin
A cloak and mask I left behind
Invoking a deep release within

A voice then gently called to me
And I followed free of fear
Keep going until you reach the light
It whispered in my ear

And so I kept a steady pace
In a direction unbeknown
All I knew with any certainty
Was I no longer felt alone

Deep within this feeling grew
From trust and love and faith
As I found myself before this light
Shining right in front my face

I reached out with a gentle hand
And the light engulfed me whole
Then filled my body with healing
That seeped deep into my soul

And when I opened my eyes again
The darkness had all but gone

In its place a gentle glow
And I felt like I belonged

It started shrinking down in size
Until a flame flickered in my palm
Despite its size, its power remained
Yet all I felt was calm

It was in this moment standing there
I felt my heart engage
A smile lit up my entire being
And I knew that things had changed

The light I held was shining bright
For all the world to see
And it was only then I realised
The shining light was me.

Silence

We believe silence to be a space of no noise
Of no distractions
No chaos
No busy-ness of being
But what if silence could be achieved in the midst of those things
In the pause you take to sip your first cup of coffee
In the exhale as you let something go
The moment you open your eyes and adjust to the morning light
Or place your feet on the ground as you get out of bed.
What if silence was a smile of happiness that just flowed through your body
and was so beautiful you couldn't help but pause to acknowledge it
The love you felt or received from someone out of the blue.
Or even a hug that comes with no words or expectations other than to
embrace you after a long and tiring day
What if there is a silence to be found in the sigh of your body as you change
into your comfy clothes, and relax at the end of a tiring days' work
Or the moment you take to say hello to a furry companion.
Perhaps there is silence in the acknowledgment of your needs and the
question you ask your body of what it desires
The space you make to stop and listen
And the action you take to gift to you
What if silence could be found in an ending, a decision to change, to move or
even to go someplace else
A mind made up and committed to something new
The feeling you get when you place your bare feet on the earth and suddenly
you feel a sense of being home
Perhaps silence is most noticeable at the end of a day, when you turn out the
lights or close your eyes before sleep.
The pause just before you slip into a space of dreams
I wonder if it is even found at the end of a chapter of a book, as you embrace
the pause before picking it up again tomorrow.
Maybe silence doesn't have to be the absence of sound or a life without
chaos
Maybe simply being present for all of it is where you find that sweet spot
The gift that shares with you a moment to notice where you are
A gift of silence that is ever present
And waiting to be enjoyed.

Everything

Each day she wakes and makes a commitment to herself. To the world.
To show up. To bring all that she can into the spaces and experiences she
creates.
Bringing all that she is into the world she walks in, the moment of now.
Some days its laughter and a sense of humour that makes others smile and
lights up her own heart.
Some days it's a love so deep it feels effortless and soul hugging, and on
others it's like holding something so delicate and precious while it heals.
There are moments where she is bursting with inspiration and ideas that all
she wants to do is dance and create and gift it to those willing to receive.
There are days where she brings her authenticity to the table so
unapologetically, it seems to activate dormant magic within her and it shines
out like a lighthouse, guiding the way for those seeking to connect.
And times her weirdness calls her out to boldly share something new and
different, even when it feels like no one is listening.
But there are also days where her magic is too much for the world, and so she
draws it in close. Saving some for herself so that she doesn't burn out. As she
allows the light to heal the overwhelm of a life spent proving her worth.
In the recharge she sits in reflection and shows up for the shadows that linger
in the dark. She painstakingly tends to the wounds of her past and nurtures
them with tenderness and care.
She battles the demons that tell her she can't or that she's too much, and she
slays them with her fierce warrior spirit. The version of her who knows her
own truth even as she rides on the back of fear.
She makes space to let her tears fall and vulnerably admit that she doesn't
always feel okay.
She owns her mistakes and the choices she's made, taking responsibility for
where she can forgive and find compassion for herself and others.
As she bounces between worlds, remembering, opening, healing, retreating,
loving, giving, expanding, breaking, growing and receiving, she shows up for
it all.
And as she looks around, she sees her sisters who are beside her doing the
same. Drawn together by the same powerful force. To seek freedom, truth
and wholeness.
As they come together and stand firm in all that they are, a magic expands
and bursts out with such an intense radiance that it's a force to be reckoned

with. Each showing up and letting others know it's safe to be seen. To be heard. To be everything that it is to be human and more.

It creates a sisterhood

A community

A family

And a power so great, that nothing can stop it from changing the world.

Loved

I surrender into love
Into its fullness and expansion
It's grit and it's grace
And everlasting wholeness
The fragility yet fierceness of its embrace
It's fleeting whisper and soul hugging intensity
Its full physicality, and nurturing, gentle touch,
Invisible yet an ever-present gift in each and every moment
Its emotional rivers and rapids of feelings
Sacred waters and healing pools
Its sweetness and pain
Its perfect imperfection
I give myself permission to let go of the limitations that no longer serve me,
Where I have feared or attached to their external conditions of worth
Once defined by the illusion of sin and separation
And instead gift myself the full experience of life
Knowing I am held
Knowing I am enough
That love flows through my veins, renewing and restoring
And continually supporting me through each cycle of death and rebirth
For I am forever birthing new parts of me into being with each beat of my
beautiful heart
Here is where I belong
Comforted by the knowing it is always there
Never separate
Never lost
Never withheld
Just waiting
Holding and nurturing
And as I surrender fully to its flow and infinite presence
I finally release my grip
No longer needing to hold on so tight
For no matter what I experience
Or where I find myself
I know I am love
And love is always loving me

Universe

To surrender and make space for growth is to be brave and courageous.
For the level of honesty and trust it asks of us, to feel into the things we often
shy away from. To hold hands with fear and keep going anyway. To make
space for energy to flow into new ideas and possibilities and pathways.
It allows for synchronicities to reveal themselves and encourages us to take
leaps of faith into unknown territory that you find you can't ignore.
It's knowing that everything has its place, its gift, its lesson and message.
When we take back control from the ego, and no longer give centre stage to
the voices that demand our attention, or set the rules on how we should be.
When space is given to the often overwhelmed and chaotic mind, and love
shown to the weary and tired heart.
We open and fall deeper into the expansiveness of possibility.
A space for replenishment and discovery.
Where our roots can deepen, our bodies can soften and the soul can be heard.
Where mother Gaia can wrap her loving arms around you and tenderly
soothe the aching in your bones.
Where the energy of life can whisper and share its wisdom and you become
part of all that is around you. Understanding the connection to all things and
that separation is merely an illusion.
We can dance with the wind as it carries sacred stories and truths, flow with
the rivers and allow the rain to wash away the old so that it can be returned to
the earth as an honouring of death and rebirth.
Sunlight helps to recharge and give back life force energy to what was once
depleted and connects you to a limitless source that can never run out.
You are part of the magic that dances between worlds.
The music of the universe
The vastness of life and creation itself.
So when you feel a call to pull back from the chaos of life. To step out of the
race and the competition.
When you feel the need to hibernate, to rest and be still for a while, and
recognise the time to plant the seeds of the life you wish to manifest. Or the
calling to grow someplace new.
Do not wait or ponder too long on the timing, your readiness or the
limitations of others that create doubt in your mind.
Allow the gentle surrendering of all that you are and all you have been up to
this moment to sink into the stillness.

Lay everything down upon the earth, bury it deep within the soil and let it find its way.

Allow all that is coming to have the freedom to move and trust in the knowing that what is true for you will never pass you by.

Recognise that deep down beneath the layers, invisible to the naked eye, important work is taking place. Honour that and cultivate patience.

Listen to the wind, take note of the songs and the signs and the guidance that is always available when you drop into your heart.

Get curious. Smile at the things that show up as if by magic. Have gratitude for the blessings that make their way to you in the form of people, conversations, gifts and inspiration.

Heed the call to seed and to grow. To bloom and to become wherever it is that you are called to go.

For a soul committed to growth, discovers that the entire universe is inside of them.

Magic

Did you know you are made of magic?
With a presence that can light a room.
A heart worth more than gold itself
Made from stardust and all things beautiful.
Filled with empathy that can soothe a troubled soul
And tears that can bathe away the heaviness of a challenging day.
And that wisdom you hold, deep in your bones, that calls out to you in the moments you forget your power.
Your strength that arises when you let the Phoenix out of its cage.
Those mighty flames that burn away what's no longer meant to stay and wings that embrace the world in a passionate hug, helping hold all the broken pieces together so they can one day heal.
The way you pour love into the cracks and watch in awe as something new takes form from what was once thought of as broken.
That longing you feel for home, for the reconnection of all souls that triggers an ever-deepening craving for unity and peace.
The way you open yourself up to be seen, like a lighthouse calling to all awakened souls to come together. And the way it inspires those who are finally ready to step up.
The bravery you muster at every unexpected twist and turn and the courage you find to crawl through the fire, to set yourself and those before you free so you may rebirth after each fall.
Do you see the foundation you have steadily built beneath your feet? Each stone carefully carved and shaped by your own bare hands.
Held together by the blood, sweat and tears that said
'I will do what it takes because I know my worth'
And with it there's the fear you bargain with on your darkest nights because you know that isn't how your story ends and so you boldly step forth into the shadows, hand in hand to seek out the joy and love you know awaits you.
The radiating glow of your aura hugs all those that step into your embrace.
Its rainbow of majestic colours in a billion different shades, showcasing your very soul in all its beauty and glory, yet still gracefully greets every other soul in their own uniqueness, merging as one to add to the pallet of ever-expanding colours and infinite possibilities.
The magnetism of your smile and your ability to hold space with such tenderness and compassion.
Those eyes that hold deep truths and speak without making a sound.

Your words that have the power to love and communicate from the very depths of your heart.
And yes, that beautiful beating heart, drumming effortlessly inside your chest, syncing with the call of the earth, the heart of Gaia herself, the universe and all of life and creation.
All of it magic
Wild, sacred, beautiful magic.
All of it is you,

Potency

What if you are not actually afraid of being judged, laughed at, made wrong, criticised, ridiculed, misunderstood or rejected.

Have you ever considered that it isn't all that you think you are not that truly frightens you?

It's all you know that you are and can be.

And it's that power and potency of the energy you carry within you that you actually fear because of what it could do if you chose to show up in the world with all of those that judge, and still be entirely you anyway.

What if that is what actually scares you most of all?

Because to do so would have the potential and power to actually change the world.

You

What if today you embraced the magic that you are and let it surprise you?
What if you embodied the miracle of what it is to be alive and the freedom it can gift you?
What if your potency was actually your superpower which gave you the ability to make changes and choices far greater than you can imagine?
What if your fears were actually the spark of excitement of stepping into something new and greater, and the possibilities that can unfold when you break though the barriers of lack and remember who you truly are?
What if you let go of the judgments of yourself that were never really yours to begin with, and asked what else can I be?
And released all judgements of others so they can be who they choose to be too?
What if you dared to make a different choice right now than the one you made ten seconds ago?
And what if that was the gateway to even more possibilities and the change you've been asking for?
What if life could come to you with such ease and joy that if you were willing to let go of everything you think you should be, and the limitations of what others have told you you can be, would change your entire life?
What spaces could open up in your world today if you were to give yourself permission to be present to everything yet attached to nothing?
What could you receive if you dropped your walls and barriers down and let the universe gift to you?
And what gift could you be to the universe and the world as a result?
What awareness could you have by allowing everything to flow through you and never harm you or your beautiful body again?
What would be possible if you allowed yourself to know what you think you don't know, and gave up the excuses that have caged you and prevented you from tapping into this inner power within?
What lives could you touch and inspire by being yourself and knowing that was enough, by recognising that you always have the choice to be something new.
That in doing so it awakened those you came into contact with to know they are enough as well, or perhaps gives them a glimpse of their own magic that they've hidden from themselves until now.
What if you were brave enough to let life as you know it fall away so that possibilities beyond your wildest dreams can show up for you, that if you

could courageously ride out the discomfort of change and let go of the things you've made significant, it would allow you to create something different that may just blow your mind?

What could you contribute to the world if you woke up today and decided to be all that you are? The magic, the potency, the space, the lightness, the consciousness, the awareness, the energy the ease and the joy that could actualise a whole new way of being.

And what if that my friend was the true gift of living.

The true gift of being you.

Soul sister

There's this lady I know and I haven't known her for long.
At least not in this lifetime.
Yet I feel like I've known her forever.
I recognised her energy the instant we met and it felt as if we were just
picking up where we left off.
In my heart I know she's the family we get to choose for ourselves, and they
are always the best kind!
She has such an incredible energy and her laughter fills a room with so much
happiness and joy that it ripples out across the universe.
Magic flows through her veins and love radiates from her being.
Her sparkle is infectious and she leaves a trail of it wherever she goes,
touching all those that are gifted with her presence, even when she doesn't
always see it herself.
She has a humour that shifts barriers with the unavoidable smiles and
laughter it creates. And the space she holds should you ever be blessed to be
held in it is like a nurturing hug from heaven.
She can break down your walls with the simplicity of a smile, one that tells
you you're safe to be you.
She'll sit with you and let you soften until it's time to find the courage to face
your fears and question what you are truly capable of.
But she also won't take any shit and will call you out when needed, nudging
you into the discomfort because she knows the magic that you hide behind
those false limitations and walls of defence.
She embraces her weirdness and uniqueness so that you too can drop the
masks you've learnt to wear.
And she dances just because she can.
Behind it all though I know there are times when she questions who she is
and forgets she doesn't always have to be that for the world. That the world
can also be that for her too.
That those around her see her light and will always remind her of it when she
has forgotten, or to offer theirs when she has burnt herself out.
To remind her what she gives and who she is every day is enough, whatever
percentage she's able to be in that moment. And they will contribute to that
with the gift of kindness she so willingly gives until she can replenish her
own cup.
In the moments she retracts to take a breath and find her truth again she
knows there is something shifting. Something brewing that's creating the
change needed for the next step of the vision she holds for the world.

And when she finds that spark watch out, because her comeback is always stronger than her setback.

There's this lady I know and I haven't known her for long,

At least not in this lifetime.

Yet she is one of the bravest and most beautiful, inspiring women I know.

Some days she has no idea of the difference she makes to those around her, just by being herself.

And just by simply being in the world.

So today I decided to remind her

Oh, and did I tell you she's made of magic!

Back to being

Change was coming.

She'd been feeling it for a while now, the sense that something was shifting. For some time she had been quietly observing with an eager yet cautious curiosity, a little unsure how it was going to show up. Or even when. For she knew those things were out of her control and had learnt that lesson the hard way.

If she allowed herself to admit it, this time though it felt different. It sparked a pang of excitement but it was overshadowed with a fear of the potency she may unleash into the world if she fully surrendered to its power. A power she had kept contained for so long.

And she wondered if the world was yet ready for such change.

She had sensed the wisps of it brewing behind the scenes for many years. Slowly forming and building as a result of the different choices she had been willing to make and the questions she found herself daring to ask. The things she had been quietly untangling herself from and letting go and the boundaries and rules of limitations she was gradually escaping.

Yet still she remained unaware of the true significance of what was occurring.

She had been in a space for too long where life had shackled her down. Where her light had been diminished to embers as too many compromises had been made and so many parts of her moulded and controlled, forcing her to slowly give up all sense of who she was.

To hide what little of her was left from all those who had rejected and tried to extinguish her light.

What they didn't know was that she had been biding her time, protecting that part of her being at all cost. All the while learning, growing, softening, shedding, and healing while she waited until she could make her move.

Until she could break free from all the prisons and limitations that had been placed upon her and had once caged her potency and magic.

Until now she had just longed to belong. To be accepted and her 'too muchness' to be loved. To know what it felt like to be truly happy rather than constantly feeling like she was in battle to prove her worth, or having to cut off more of who she was to satisfy those around her.

One day however this changed. It was so sudden in the midst of the chaos, pain and willingness to finally let herself break open, and it was the beginning of all that was to come. Instead of a need to be validated anymore, she finally decided to choose her fucking self. To love all that she was, all that she had been and all that she knew she had the potential to become.

All that time spent in the dark had given her space to face her demons and be for herself the love she had so often craved. To craft her magic, to play with the many ways she longed to create and inspire and to create such a sacred space within her which she gifted to her light so it could grow again. She made it so powerful that no demon would ever be able to find her.

It had ignited a roaring courage in her to keep going as she now understood what was happening. That their judgement, and her own, had in fact been a gift. It had become the catalyst of her undoing, her unravelling and her awakening so that she could now shed all that had been placed upon her by others, and the armour she had once forged to play safe and small. To protect what light had remained.

The space and freedom it created allowed the embers she had been so carefully protecting to spark and re-ignite, lighting the way back up to the surface. Up through the layers of the earth from where she had planted herself some time ago.

As she began to rise, she could feel the slightest push from beneath her body, as if the earth was giving her a gentle nudge of encouragement. It was nurturing yet quietly persistent.

She smiled, bemused by its attempt at subtlety, yet grateful for the gift it was offering as if it was letting her know it believed in her too.

As it all began to intensify, as she called more of herself back into being, all the parts of her she had once abandoned and rejected, she knew there was no going back.

It was time, and she knew she was ready, despite the bubbling of fear that relentlessly gnawed at her as she wondered how the world would receive her in her wholeness.

She knew this was what she'd been waiting for as she got a sense of the lifetimes she had spent planning for this very moment.

With each change that occurred and as more layers of the self she thought she was or had had to be fell away, it took all her strength to release her grip and surrender them. To let her reality shatter over and over as it stripped away lifetimes of conditioning, lies and things that had never truly belonged to her.

She felt the earth shudder as it engulfed the pain she had been carrying for millennia, and all that of the generations of ancestors who had been before her. It honoured the healing she was now willing to allow, and the needless suffering she was finally ready to acknowledge and let go.

She found herself stripped bare so that she could see all that she had been choosing and hanging onto. Once thinking it was all she could ever be. The layers of limitations and judgements that had built up a fortress of walls around her weary yet fiercely loving heart.

A heart that always knew she was here to do more, and carried deep within it the vision of what the world could be one day, patiently waiting for when that day would come.

And so, as her walls fell and crumbled down, in the destruction of letting go, she began to notice a very different yet strangely familiar energy around her.

It could only be described as a lightness, as though her body was somehow floating to the surface now rather than fighting it. It created a space to breathe and to be and she found herself expanding further and further out into its vastness. Following it with a childlike curiosity to explore just how far it reached, as it willed her to bring all of her into this space. In doing so she discovered there were in fact no limits, no boundaries, and no end. Nothing but infinite creative possibilities where all of her could be and be free.

She softened into a sense of ease, despite the raw uncertainty and unknown of what was taking place. There were no words to describe it, for in doing so would solidify what was occurring and she sensed its need to move freely and to dance.

That this creative force required her to surrender in a way she never had before, her mind having no place in this transition.

In what felt like a life time yet no time at all, the ground gave way above her and she broke free. The emergence was disorientating yet surprisingly orgasmic as the light caressed her face and helped her body to soften and unfurl with ease.

With her feet now standing upon the earth, her constant companion, a dear friend, it held her up like a proud mother until she was ready to take her first steps.

She was a little unsure how she would adjust to the world, or perhaps how the world would adjust to her.

She was no longer who she was, or who the world had once required or demanded her to be. But she was also not quite all she knew she could be. For there was no fun in knowing that.

So, in the space of presence with her new surroundings, simply being was what she chose. Each moment allowed her to wonder what else she could choose next and what magic that would create. It was inspiring and lit up her imagination beyond what she had ever known.

As she gained her balance and began to move out into the world, she sensed the adventures that awaited. The people she would meet and the fun she could have. Her steps were light and her body moved in a way it never had before, healthy and unburdened from the pain and the lies that had once buried her. With each footstep she kissed the earth in gratitude for never giving up on her, and found comfort in its unending presence.

She had no idea what exactly awaited her, only that it was there, everywhere, all around her and in everything. She could feel it calling to her, like a child waiting to play. It made her smile and just the warmth of that gesture lit up her whole being. For in that moment, she knew this was happiness.

It felt so good that she promised to gift it to herself every day, and to share it with anyone who crossed her path and was willing to receive it.

It was as though she could finally see for the first time. Her vision clearer than it had ever been. The awareness it gave her was almost overwhelming in a strange yet beautiful way. Because not only could she now see the true beauty and magic and possibilities around her, she could also more deeply perceive how colourless and limited the world was to so many who walked upon it.

The lies that kept so many asleep and unaware of the choices they could make and all they had the potential to be.

She knew that she could not change this with force. Nor did she find she had any desire too, for she had spent far too long trying to be the saviour. There was no longer any judgement of what they were choosing. She no longer felt a need to save or to rescue or even interfere. Instead, she found peace in knowing now why she was here and what she was meant to do next. Every day from then on, she chose to wake up and 'be' the ease and joy in the world. She chose kindness, she chose love, she chose awareness, she chose gratitude, she chose peace and she chose everything that made her sweet body feel light and everything that opened up new doors of possibilities to explore.

On the days she found herself tested as the world attempted to pull her back into its grip, she paused and let her energy expand out. She let it flow effortlessly through her like a river, filled with gratitude for its gift of awareness and the potency it allowed her to tap into in order to change its form. Then she took a deep breath and effortlessly made another choice. One that always brought her back to being again and gave her the freedom she now knew existed and would never give up again.

She sought out other beings that shared the other pieces of a new world vision, and rejoiced in the blessings, love, weirdness, potency and contribution that they could all be for one another. Those who also knew of the magic that flowed through the veins of the earth, danced in every cell and molecule and spread infinitely across the universe.

She met beings that moved her in ways she hadn't expected. She found soul family that lit up her world with such love and a sense of home. She created connections and reunited with her tribe who shattered any remains of what she had ever thought friendship or love to be and who opened her heart to even greater depths of oneness.

She knew this had been a long time coming. It was everything and so much more than she had expected it to be and yet she knew there was way more to come that would surprise her. So much more to create and explore.

So much more to be.

It was time

And this, was just the beginning…

Walking home

Life brings us many experiences.

Many people walk through our lives at various points and times

They can touch our hearts with profound kindness and show up in moments we forget who we are; to show us the light that they see and mirror it back for us to remember again.

Often serving as a reminder that we are all connected by love.

They can bring a sense of joy and a wondrous laughter that literally lightens up your world.

And create a smile so big that it bubbles from the inside, slowly forming from the very depths of your soul and beams out like a radiating rainbow of light.

They can knock on your door and invite you to a party you never want to leave, showing you just how amazing and joyful life can be through the gift of true connection and togetherness.

At the same time, there are those who can also show up to create great change and inspire significant growth. Who shatter the world and life as you knew it to be, to create a tornado of chaos that paves the way for a whole new chapter to begin.

They force you to change what you had become too comfortable with, revealing the limitations and walls you had once built to keep your potency and power contained.

They can burst a bubble of momentary bliss and leave without a goodbye. Taking with them a piece of your heart.

People can challenge you in ways you may wonder if you will ever come back from.

And ignite emotions like a flame to a fuse.

We engage and navigate through these phases of lightness and dark, hoping it's worth the pain and sometimes wishing for joy to stay a little while longer. Wondering if it's possible to have both and yet still remain true to who you are.

We can have moments where we are surrounded by the most amazing people and yet somehow feel utterly alone. Those times of solitude where you wish you could reach out, or that someone will come find you curled up in the darkness that came to visit so unexpectedly.

Even just to hold your hand while you let the tears fall and find your way back again. For in that moment you realise that you once thought you wanted to disappear, but what you actually wanted was to be found.

To be seen, to be acknowledged and to be loved.
And to know that you deserve those things.
At times there is a loneliness that can engulf you in a wave of grief so huge you fear you won't ever be able to resurface.
But then through the chaos a hand appears, offered out for you to take hold. And that grip feels like a million hugs over. Shattering any illusions you once had of being alone. It offers connection and a reminder we are always held, even in the moments we least expect it to show up, or need it most. Often by the most unexpected of people.
Yet these are the kind who also gift you something far more precious. A space in which you come to find *yourself*, rather than actually needing to be found. And they hold that space with such love, tenderness and a lack of judgement that you finally feel safe to be all that you are.
We each walk varying roads, discovering who we can be and what our purpose is. We are all on our way to get someplace, stopping along the way to help, guide, encourage, support or love one another.
To gift a smile, a bit of warmth, wisdom or a touch of magic.
Some of these people stay a while, and some, if you are lucky, remain for a lifetime and those are the ones to truly treasure. The rare ones that face the seasons with you. Hand in hand you brave the storms together, holding space for you to be nothing other than yourselves, however many times that changes.
There are those too who just pay a fleeting visit as they drop through, who pass like a ghost in the night and often create a quick or important change, or simply leave a gift of a compliment that warms your weary heart.
Each contributes to where we are going, in some way or another. Through the good, the bad and the ugly. The highs, the lows, the triumphs and the tears, and everything in between.
All of us in it together.
All just walking each other home.

For you

Yes you, dear reader.
What will it take to nurture you?
To give back to you?
To forgive you and all the versions of you, you have been?
To stand up for you
To know you are important?
And also worthy. Ten times over.
To accept you are deserving of the true joy of living?
And to gift yourself a life of happiness and love.
What will it take for you to dance and set yourself free?
To take up space so unapologetically.
To show up in the world as you are?
Exactly as you are.
And to open up to all you can be?
What will it take dear soul
To choose you?
And to love yourself the way you were always meant to?

~~The End~~

What else is possible now?

Acknowledgements

Special thanks to the people who have helped me over the years to awaken and discover my magic. Who have loved and accepted me for who I am and all the different versions of me as I have grown and changed on this journey. For loving me at my best but also loving me even more at my worst. Through the messy tears, the grief, the heartache, lows, losses and everything in between. For being there to celebrate my wins, cheering me on and for keeping me going, especially on the days I was ready to give up. For your knowledge, wisdom, honesty, patience, healing, friendship, love and support.

I love you all and I have such an immense amount of gratitude for the kindness you have shared and the difference you have all made to my life in different ways, simply by being you.

To Lisa, Amanda, Ulla, Marilyn, Fiona S, Lexi, Susie, Claire, Suzanne, Kelly, Caz, Fiona B, Christine, Sarah-Jayne, CK friends, Theresa and so many more.

To my late grandma and grandad, my mum and dad and my family.

Thank you
Xxx

Thank you also to Jane for sharing your time, energy, wisdom and skills. For proof reading and editing this book for me which has finally enabled me to bring a long awaited dream into fruition, to birth it into the world and officially publish my first book!

Dedications

To Theresa, for your persistent yet gentle nudge of encouragement which has prompted me to be brave enough finally share my work with the world. And to allow myself to be seen regardless of the judgements I have grown up with. That it is finally time to stop hiding and playing small and instead to share my voice and my magic, because there are people in the world who it can truly inspire and touch. You are one of those rare gems that has shown up in my life and changed it for the better, changed me for the better, or perhaps simply allowed me to be nothing other than myself and who I've always been beneath the masks I thought I had to wear. You are a gift I will forever treasure. I love you and the poem 'soul sister' in this book is dedicated to you as a reminder of the magic that you are.

To Susie, you came into my life when I was all but ready to give up and showed me what friendship truly is. We have walked together on this journey hand in hand for the last few years, held each other up, laughed, cried and cheered each other on through some of our most challenging and difficult times. I genuinely wouldn't be where I am now without your constant love, patience, friendship and support. 'Walking home' was inspired by you and so may it serve as a reminder of the difference you make in the world, simply by being in it and being you.

And lastly, (though I could dedicate this to so many more)
To my Grandad Joe. For being my guiding light from the other side, igniting my spiritual journey and giving me the strength to make some of the toughest decisions of my life. But most importantly for reminding me that I am never truly alone. I love you.
Always.

xxx

Recommended reading

You can heal your life by Louise Hay
Energy Medicine by Donna Eden
Becoming the one by Sheleana Aiyana
Being you changing the world by Dr Dain Heer
Body Whispering by Dr Dain Heer
The Celestine Prophecy by James Redfield
Existential Kink by Carolyn Elliott
Conversations with God by Neale Donald Walsch
The way of the tracker by Carrie Jost
The universe has your back by Gabrielle Bernstein
The untethered soul by Michael A Singer

About the Author

Gabriella is currently working on ideas for book number two! Training at practitioner level of Creative Kinesiology and transitioning into doing more of what she loves and what lights her up each and every day. Baby plans are still on the cards one day when the opportunity presents itself. For now she is simply trusting where she is meant to be.

She currently lives in Cornwall with her family and two beautiful cat companions, surrounded by the most amazing and incredible friends, and is loving the freedom of discovering more about who she can be each day when she chooses to be herself. And from there what else is truly possible.

Printed in Great Britain
by Amazon

37021453R00059